TBH, Too Much Drama

Also by Lisa Greenwald

TBH, Too Much Drama

KT KATHERINE TEGEN BOOKS
An Imprint of HarperCollins Publishers

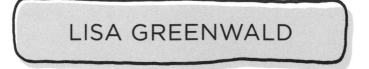

LISA GREENWALD

Katherine Tegen Books is an imprint of HarperCollins Publishers.

TBH, Too Much Drama
Copyright © 2019 by Lisa Greenwald
Emoji icons provided by EmojiOne
Photo on page 55 © 2019 by NAKphotos/Getty Images
Photo on page 89 © 2019 by Nicola Bertolini/Shutterstock
All rights reserved. Manufactured in U.S.A. No part of this book may be used or reproduced in any manner whatsoever without written permission except in the case of brief quotations embodied in critical articles and reviews. For information address HarperCollins Children's Books, a division of HarperCollins Publishers, 195 Broadway, New York, NY 10007.
www.harpercollinschildrens.com
ISBN 978-0-06-268996-2
Typography by Aurora Parlagreco
19 20 21 22 LSCC 10 9 8 7 6 5 4 3 2
❖
First Edition

For the Rosenberg crew—Aaron, Karen, Ari, Sharon, Ezra, Maayan, Elon, and Andrew

PEEP SQUAD 4 LIFE

PRIANKA

Guysssss pls hold bus 4 me 🙏

GABRIELLE

Again, Pri? 😂 🙀 🙀

PRIANKA

Couldn't find penguin pjs & now I'm
soooooooo late 😫 😫 😫

CECILY

Holding but hurry 🏃

GABRIELLE

I am sooooooo excited it's spirit week 😎
😍 😻

Have been waiting my whole life 4 this

PRIANKA

4 real, Gabs? LOL 😂 😂

1

GABRIELLE

Yes 4 real 👍

CECILY

LOL

PRIANKA

Can't wait to see ur pjs 😎 😎

From: Mr. Carransey, Principal, Yorkville Middle School
To: All Middle School Students, Parents, Faculty, Staff
Subject: SPIRIT WEEK IS HERE!

Dear Yorkville Middle School Community:

As you know, Spirit Week is here! The last week of school. The final days of the academic year.

It is a happy, fun, joyous, celebratory time!

However, we must make sure it is a safe time as well—both in person and online. Above all, we must be kind to one another. Let's remember all the lessons we have learned.

Day 1 = pajama day + trivia bowl + campfire lunch day!

See attached for our FULL SPIRIT WEEK SCHEDULE! WOO!

Have fun!
Principal Carransey

Be the change you want to see in the world.
—Gandhi

SPIRIT WEEK SCHEDULE

MONDAY:
Pajama Day
Trivia Bowl
Cookout Campfire Lunch

TUESDAY:
College Day
Tug-of-War
Locker Cleanout
Creative Sandwiches Lunch

WEDNESDAY:
Singdown
Finals Pass-Back
Color War Relay
Optional Fence-Painting Project + Pizza

THURSDAY:
Bagel Breakfast
Team Community Service Morning
Early Dismissal aka Take-a-Break Day

FRIDAY:
LAST DAY OF SCHOOL
Turn in Computers
Charades

SILVER GIRLS 4 EVA

VICTORIA

OMG I LOVE PAJAMAS 🌑 💤 🖤 🤍 💜

I kinda wish we all matched like M girls do

CECILY

True but I HAD 2 wear these flamingo shorty pjs 👍👍

I luv them so much 🐱🐱🐱

GABRIELLE

And Pri is obsessed w/ her penguin ones 🐧🐧🐧

And these zebra stripy capris r my fave 😍

VICTORIA

Omg u r all animals 🐶🐱🐫🐱🐧🐤🦢 🐓🕊️🦃

GABRIELLE

Not on purpose I swear 🙀 💁 🙈 🙊

VICTORIA

I am the only rainbow 🌈🌈🌈🌈

CECILY

Sooo that means.......

We r noah's ark theme ⛅☂🌧🌧🏳 🌈

Animals + rainbow 👏 👏 👏

VICTORIA

Ooooh 👏 👏 👏

GABRIELLE

OMG YES ❗💚 🎲 💚 🎲

VICTORIA

Ur a genius 🚨 💡 🔦

CECILY

Pays 2 pay attention in Sunday school 🏫 🏫 🏫

PRIANKA

LOL 😂 😂

We all look super fab 👭👭👭👭

Don't 4get campfire cooking day guysssss
🏕️🏕️🔥🔥

VICTORIA

Will help u all get ready 4 ur camping trip
🏕️

GABRIELLE

True but it's weird we r all just randomly
gonna cook in the woods behind school
🌲🌳🌴

PRIANKA

It'll be cool 😎 😎 😎 Gabs

U gotta get over ur weird camping phobia
before we go LOL 😲 😲

GABRIELLE

Ok 👈👍😫🚫😳😲

1st bell just rang 🔔🔔🔔

Phones away 📱 📱 📱 📱

VICTORIA

Luv how we text when we r right next 2 each other 🙅🙅🙅

CECILY

It is a little weird tho 🙈🙈🙈

PRIANKA

I feel like peeps r always eavesdropping so texting is safer 👂👂

GABRIELLE

Not really cuz we know parents always snoop on our phones LOL 💼👩💼👩

CECILY

NOTHING IS SAFE

Dun dun dun 🎹🎹🎹

VICTORIA

Hahahahahahahah 😆 😂

GABRIELLE

K phones away 4 real now

I c hall monitor coming 👀 👀 👀

PRIANKA

Smooooches 💋 💋 💋 💋 💋

From: Mr. Akiyama, Vice Principal, Yorkville Middle School
To: All Middle School Students
Subject: Surprise addition to Spirit Week!

Hi, all!

Spirit Week is off to a great start! But we want to add one more (optional) activity!

Please submit an essay (no more than 500 words) highlighting your reflections on the school year. The winner will receive a $100 gift certificate to Jennie's Pizza. Yum!

Good luck!

Mr. Akiyama

#YORKVILLEUNITED

Individually, we are one drop. Together, we are an ocean.—Ryunosuke Satoro

SILVER GIRLS 4 EVA

P C G V

PRIANKA

Guyssssss how insane was that trivia bowl ⁉️⁉️⁉️⁉️

Why does Jared act like such a know it all 🤓🤓🤓🤓🤓🤓🤓🤓🤓🤓🤓

CECILY

IDK but he really does

GABRIELLE

He got so many answers right tho ✔️☑️✔️ ☑️✔️☑️✔️☑️✔️☑️✔️☑️✔️☑️✔️☑️

PRIANKA

IK but he's so braggy 👎👎👎👎

VICTORIA

Not complaining bc my team won wooooooo hooooooo 🎉🎉🎉🎉

Good 2 have Jared around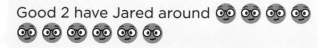

CECILY

Haha same 👊 👊 👊

PRIANKA

Blargh 2 u, Vic 😬 🙄 😬 🙄

CECILY

Guys I snapped a pic of the beans my team made @ the campfire cookout 🙄 📷 📷 🤳

Ur so lucky ur on other teams 🍀 🍀 🍀

We may have won trivia bowl but I was stuck making this

Y did we get the grossest thing 😖 😖 😝

GABRIELLE
EWWWWWWWWW 💩 💩 💩

PRIANKA
R team's shish kebabs were really good
👍 👍

GABRIELLE
Vic, did u like r tinfoil hamburgers 🍔 🍔
🍔 🍔

VICTORIA
They were OK OK

GABRIELLE
Yeah not bad

Glad we r on same team 🐺 🐺 🐺 🐺

VICTORIA
Me 2 🙌 🙌 🙌

13

PRIANKA

R u all on 🚌 🚌 🚌 now

Forgot 2 tell u my mom is picking me up 4 bal vihar meeting 4 next yr even tho we have bal vihar party this week toooooooo 😩 🐱 😩 🐱

VICTORIA

Oh yeah Arjie said he was going 2 that 😍 😍 😍 😍

GABRIELLE

Arjie LOL

Ur still totes in 😻 😻 😻 😻 Vic

VICTORIA

Yuppppppppp 💞 🖤 🤍 💖 💘 🖤

Will miss him sooo much when I'm in philly all summer & miss u guys too obv 😩 😳 😩 😳

But I'm excited to b w/ Nic & Kim 👭 👭 👭 & my grandma LOL 😂 😂

14

GABRIELLE

Hahahahahahahahah

Pri, we r all on 🚌 🚌 🚌

CECILY

Wondered where u were 😼 😺 😸

PRIANKA

This is COMO 4 real 😭 🙀 😭

VICTORIA

What is COMO

PRIANKA

Like FOMO but since I'm actually missing out...

Crying over missing out 🙀 🙀 🙀 😭 🥺

GABRIELLE

LOL 😁 😂

PRIANKA

JK I'm not really crying but can we make COMO a thing

CECILY

Sure, on it! ☑ ✔

GABRIELLE

Same

VICTORIA

I will be COMO all summer 😪 🙄 🙄 😿 😿 👇 👇

555-55

YORKVILLE MIDDLE SCHOOL TEXT ALERT: Reminder to all students that all school laptops must be turned in by Friday at three p.m.

PEEP SQUAD 4 LIFE

(P) (C) (G)

PRIANKA

SILVER GIRLS 4 EVA

(P) (C) (G) (V)

GABRIELLE

Vic, can u text me the pic of all of us in pjs

I want my dad 2 print for me

PRIANKA

Text 2 me 2 plsss 🙏 🙏

CECILY

Same

VICTORIA

On it 👐👐💓🩶🖤

BTW did I tell u my philly friends r coming 2morrow 2 visit for a few days 🐰🐰

They finished school last week 🐧🐧

PRIANKA

OMG that is so fun 👏👏👏

CECILY

So excited 2 meet them 👧👧👧👧👧👧

GABRIELLE

R they participating in spirit week 2 LOL 😼😼😼

VICTORIA

Yessssss 🏆🏆

CECILY

So fun 😎😎

18

VICTORIA

Im soooo excited 4 them to meet u guys & Arjie of course 😍😍😍😍😼😼😼😼

CECILY

LOL, Vic

U crack me up 😛😊😝😜

R u guys doing the essay contest 📕📘📗📙

I am ☑✔

GABRIELLE

Me 2 🖐🖐

PRIANKA

IDK kinda over schoolwork 🚫🚫🚫🚫🚫

VICTORIA

LOL 4 real - no thank u essayyyyyy 😿😿

GABRIELLE

LOL, Vic, u r really funny 😹😹😹😹

VICTORIA

Thanksssssssssss 🙀🙀

Stand by for pic

• • •

UGH pic won't send 😡😡🙀

will try 2morrow ✌️

LYL 🤍 🤍 💔 🖤 ❤️

GABRIELLE

Xoxo 🖤 🖤 🖤

PRIANKA

Bue

LOL BYE ✋ 😲 😲 😲

CECILY

Bue bue lol mwah 😽😽

ESSAY CONTEST

REFLECTIONS ON THE SCHOOL YEAR

by Cecily Anderson

First draft

I'm going to be honest here. The thing that enticed me most about this contest was the gift card to Jennie's. The best pizza in the world, in my opinion, and we are so lucky to have it in our town. Our beloved Yorkville. But anyway. I also like writing. So here goes. I think it was a very ~~awkward~~ ~~hard~~ interesting school year. It was my first year in middle school and I didn't know what to expect. It had many ups and downs but I think our school community became stronger over the course of the year. We struggled with bullying and learning how to behave with phones and I think we really grew.

SILVER GIRLS 4 LIFE

CECILY

This essay is really hard 😒 😟

PRIANKA

Exactly y I'm not doing it 😹 😹 😹 😹

CECILY

4 real tho

GABRIELLE

It is hard ughhhhh 🙀 🙀 🙀 🙀

I may skip it 😬

PRIANKA

Time 2 unwindddddd guyysssss 👙 ☀️ 🍉

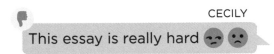

No more work or stress 🚫 🚫 🚫 🚫 🚫 😬
😬 😬

VICTORIA

Agree

Cecily, Mara

C M

CECILY

R u doing the essay contest 📕

MARA

I think so but IDK

U ?

CECILY

Same sooo hard 🐶🐶🐶🐶

I thought I had lots of ideas but now IDK 😭

MARA

Haha me 2

We are already out of school mode ya know

CECILY

IK but it's only been a few days

MARA

True

CECILY

Soooo happy we don't have summer hw 👏👏✊💪✊

MARA

Me 2 OMG

I hate summer hw

CECILY

What r u wearing for college day tomw

MARA

My parents met @ U of Mich so wearing a tee from there

U?

CECILY

Well my mom went to Notre Dame & my dad went 2 Duke so IDK

MARA

Do u have ND top & Duke shorts? LOL

CECILY

Hahahaha pos will check 😼😼😼😼

Does that seem like 2 much

MARA

I don't think so haha

CECILY

K cool‼‼

C u tomw 😿😿

MARA

Gnight xo

CECILY

Nite!

SILVER GIRLS 4 LIFE

GABRIELLE

Guys, check out this meme I made

I had such bad writers block trying 2 do the essay contest

So I did this instead

I saw a thing online that said take weirdest pic some1 sent to u & make a meme

Sounded fun

WHEN CAMPFIRE FOOD IS BETTER THAN THE YORKVILLE CAFETERIA

THIS WAS GROSS.
YORKVILLE CAF IS WORSE.

CECILY

OMG is that my picture 🙀🙀🙀🙀

GABRIELLE

LOL yes 👌👌👌

Weirdest pic I have

PRIANKA

Hahahha, Gabs 😼😼

VICTORIA

How do u make a meme ❓

Will show u next time we hang

LOL ok 👍

From: Diana Katz
To: Manjula Basak, Elizabeth Anderson
Subject: Bra shopping?

In the words of our dear daughters, OMG!!!! But I think the time has come. Gabby needs more than the tank top she wears under her clothes every day. Can we all do this together and get them some, um, support at Great Shapes? Brace ourselves for the agony? I remember when I went with my mom and it was pure hell. Or am I being dramatic? Help. Longing for the days when our biggest worry was how long the afternoon nap would be.

X Diana

Colin, Gabrielle

Yo check out this meme I made

> WHEN CAMPFIRE FOOD
> IS BETTER THAN THE
> YORKVILLE CAFETERIA
>
> THIS WAS GROSS.
> YORKVILLE CAF IS WORSE.

COLIN

Hahahahahahahahahah

That is so funny

So happy we didn't have to make those beans

GABRIELLE

IK

COLIN

How did u get that pic

GABRIELLE

Cece sent to me

COLIN

So funny

She was on beans team

GABRIELLE

Yup

Unknown, Gabrielle

UNKNOWN

Gabrielle, is this ur #

What u did was so rude

GABRIELLE

??

Who is this

UNKNOWN

Jared

GABRIELLE

Which Jared

MAYBE: JARED

Remington

We worked hard on those beans

Why did u write a mean meme

GABRIELLE

It was just a joke

MAYBE: JARED

It wasn't funny

GABRIELLE

Ok

I'm sorry

Colin sent 2 u

MAYBE: JARED

Yes

Bye

Prianka, Gabrielle

GABRIELLE

Pri, Jared is bugging about my meme 🙀🙀😮😨

Saying it's so mean & stuff

PRIANKA

Whatever it was a joke 😜😜

NBD @ all 🙂😀😁🙂😎

GABRIELLE

Agree ✔✔

Every1 is cray 😵😵😨😲🙈🙅

PRIANKA

Agree ⚡⚡

Dear Diary . . . too tired to write today.

I ♡ where I live.

Colin, Gabrielle

GABRIELLE

Colin, u can't just send something out w/o permission

Y did u do that

COLIN

I only sent 2 Jared & he didn't send 2 any1

Is this a group chat

GABRIELLE

No dummy just us

I wud not be that stupid

COLIN

Y r u buggin

GABRIELLE

Cuz I'm nervous & I want to make sure nothing bad is on my comp b4 we turn them in

COLIN

Ok but ur phone isn't ur comp

GABRIELLE

I know but iMessages come up on both

So we could get in big trouble

COLIN

Chill

GABRIELLE

Whatever bye

COLIN

Bye

CAMPING OMG SO SOON WHATTTTTT

P C G

CECILY

Guys what r u writing 4 secret fact 4 camping trip mixer thing 😖

GABRIELLE

Ummm that I can wiggle my 👂 👂 👂 I think

CECILY

Good one ✓ ☑

Pri?

PRIANKA

That I own 13 saris? 👊 👊 👊 💚

CECILY

That's so 😎 COOL 😎 COOL

I got nothing 0 0 0

37

GABRIELLE

That u were 6th grade rep?

CECILY

Eh 👧😦👧

GABRIELLE

❗

Oh! That u still sleep with Patches 🐶🐩
🐶🐩

CECILY

Is that babyish 👶👶👶🍼🍼🍼

PRIANKA

No it's so cute

Esp bc ur mom's BFF from college made
him 👵👵👵👵👩👩

It's a cool story 😎😎😎😎

CECILY

Ok ☑

He is cute rite 🐶🐩🐶🐩🐱🐱😻😻😻😻

PRIANKA

OMG yessss so cute 😍😍

GABRIELLE
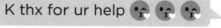
We all 💜💜💜 Patches

CECILY

K thx for ur help 😘😘😘

SILVER GIRLS 4 LIFE

P C G V

GABRIELLE

Guyssss I'm obsessed w/ making memes

CECILY

OMG, Gabs, whatttt ⁉️⁉️

GABRIELLE

Just 4 fun, Cece

Don't worry 🙂 😐 😁 😆

CECILY

Feels kinda mean 😵 😵 😲 😲 😦 🙁 😐

GABRIELLE

No u know I 😻😻😾😻😾😻 you

PRIANKA

Kinda funny, Gabs

Cece, it's NBD to 😵😫🛏️ 💤 with a stuffed animal

CECILY

K fine whatever

VICTORIA

I get how Cecily feels

It is kinda private 😬 🙄

But whatevs it's just us ●● 👓 🕶️

CECILY

K true gtg bye 😗 😗

41

CODE RED HELP ME NOW

P C G

GABRIELLE

U guys this is code red mama drama
😲 😲 😲

CECILY

!??

Getting ready 4 school 🎒 🎒 🎒

Discuss on bus 🚌 🚌 🚌

GABRIELLE

2 private 2 discuss on bus 🙅

Text discuss & then delete text k?

PRIANKA

??

GABRIELLE

My mom left her phone on the counter and
I saw an email.... 📲

???

GABRIELLE

She emailed ur moms bout bra shopping 🐨🐨🐨🐨

Like all of us 2gether 😫😲😧😬

Ahhhhhhhhhh

PRIANKA

OMG why 😣😣😣

GABRIELLE

Can't even type this

Too 😱😧😱

CECILY

K don't stress

After we get off bus we go to single stall b-room by drama wing 🎭

Discuss in private

PRIANKA

K hahaha drama wing for OUR DRAMA
LOL 🎭 🎭 🎭

Honestly tho this feels scary 🐺 🐺 🐺 but
will end up being NBD 🧜‍♀️

GABRIELLE

IDK, Pri, but ok 👌 👌

CODE RED HELP ME NOW

(P) (C) (G)

CECILY

K guys we need 2 be @ tug o war in 5 min
⏱ 🕐 ⏳

But so glad we talked about the code red
sitch

PRIANKA

Same

GABRIELLE

If we gotta do it, at least we can do it 2gether ya know

CECILY

True ☑ ✔

Do we let on that we know they talked about this ‼⁇‼

PRIANKA

IDK

GABRIELLE

I don't think so

1st one that 👂 👂 👂 about it from mom tells the others k?

PRIANKA

K

CECILY

I'm gonna look @ great shapes website and pick bras & email 2 u so we can be in and out of there as fast as pos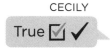

45

We will know what 2 get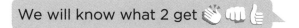

GABRIELLE

Smart Cece

CECILY

K we gotta go

Put away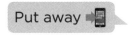

PRIANKA

K bye

GABRIELLE

Mwah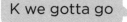

Colin, Gabrielle

COLIN

Got any more memes

This locker cleanout is sooo boring

GABRIELLE

LOL it is

NOT SENDING U ANY MORE MEMES

COLIN

Ok

Back 2 cleanout

Prob should've cleaned once during the year

GABRIELLE

LOL bye

SILVER GIRLS 4 LIFE

P C G V

VICTORIA

Hi friendsssssss

How is every1 enjoying these creative sandwiches 🙄🙄🙄

I feel bad my friends r experiencing this weirdo lunch 😫😫😫🍔🥘

PRIANKA

LOL my team made bologna & fluff and then avocado & fluff for vegetarians 😷😷🤢💩💩💩

VICTORIA

Ewwwww we made tuna and pickles 🐠🐡🐡

I thought that was bad 😭😢😆😂😁

So funny 😂 😄 😂 😄

Ours was actually super good 😊 😊 😊 😊

Sprouts + turkey + mayo + mustard + mozzarella 🥪 🦃 🥪 🦃

PRIANKA

Yummmmmmmm 🍀 🍀 🍀

VICTORIA

Gabs, Colin was talking about ur meme

GABRIELLE

Huh? 😧 😐 🙀

VICTORIA

The beans one 🤭 😝

GABRIELLE

Oh LOL 😂

VICTORIA

He thinks ur so funny 😊 🙂 🙃 😏 😌 😍 💜

Cecily, Mara

C M

MARA

Sorry I couldn't hang after school 2day

Had a doc appt b4 sleepaway camp

Blargh

CECILY

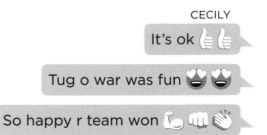

It's ok 👍👍

Tug o war was fun 😍😍

So happy r team won 💪👊👏

Also so happy we r on same team 4 spirit week obvs 👧👧👧👧

MARA

Me 222222222

Except for the beans LOL

CECILY

Yeah ewwwww

When do u leave 4 camp 🏕️ 🏕️ 🏕️

MARA

Next wknd sooooo excited

CECILY

Woo hoo 🎉 🎉 🎉 🎉

I will write 2 u 💌 💌 💌

MARA

We need 2 hang b4 we leave 4 summer

CECILY

 4 sure

Come over 4 s'mores in my backyard tomw night? 🔥 🔥 🔥

MARA

Oooh sounds fab

CECILY

K bye smooches

MARA

Smooches

Dear Diary,

When Aunt Sheila gave you to me, I didn't realize how important you would become. I'm sorry if that seems mean. I just never expected to be a Diary Person. Ya know? Anyway, I guess we are always changing.

That brings me to something super secret and private that I have literally not told a single person and I don't even know if I can write down. It's not a bad thing at all. It's just new and kind of surprising. For me. Anyway.

So here goes. I feel like I finally have a crush. At least based on how my friends describe a crush. But it's not on a boy. It's actually on Mara. My neighbor.

How crazy is that? Not because she's a girl—because it's totally fine to like girls if you're a girl or boys if you're a boy. Whatever. But crazy because she's my neighbor and my friend and it kind of happened out of nowhere.

Like I find myself thinking about her before I go to sleep, and wondering what she's doing. And her hair is so pretty—it's like half brown and half blond and it curls up on the bottom. I don't think she even tries to get it that way. And she's just so nice and she has the funniest laugh.

UGH. I do have a crush, right? OMG. I wish you could answer me.

Love,
Cecily

BRA SHOPPING PREP OMG

P   C   G

CECILY

Guys I did research on great shapes site ⌨️ 💻 🖥️ 💻

I found a few cute bras that are ok and not 2 crazy

Is it awk if we all have same bra LOL 😳 😳

PRIANKA

● ● ●

GABRIELLE

No totes fine 🙆 🙆 🙆 💁

PRIANKA

Agree send us the pic

GABRIELLE

So let's just go in & say we all want this one & get out, k? 😡 😼 😼

CECILY

That's the plan 🏆 💯 👌

PRIANKA

K cool 👍 👊 🤏 👌

OMG COMPS 😱 😨

VICTORIA

Guys did u hear that reminder
announcement after school about comps
🙀 🙀 😳 😨 😳 😨 😳 😨

Jamal Parker told me he is volunteering for
tech dept and helping 2 check all comps
⌨️ 🖥️ 🖥️ 🖥️

Every 1 will be checked for inappropriate
stuff 😨 😨 😨

Can they see ur chats ⁉️

I haven't used comps 4 anything besides
school stuff since I got in so much trouble
📵 🚫 ⛔ 🙈 🙊 🙉

Worried 4 u guys tho 😳 😨

56

Ack IDK 🙀 🙀 🙀 🙀 🙀

PRIANKA

IDK either 👩 ▪️ 👩

We didn't say anything that bad did we
🙊 ▪️ 🙊

GABRIELLE

Who is a tech genius
🖥️ 🖥️ 🖥️ 🖥️ 🖥️ 🖥️ 🖥️ 🖥️ 🖥️ 🖥️ 🖥️

VICTORIA

Ummm

I didn't think we would have 2 give comps
back @ end of year 🖥️ 🖥️

CECILY

Me neither

PRIANKA

I heard they r updating all of them &
handing out again in Sept 👩

GABRIELLE

Oh

I don't think there is anything that bad on mine

VICTORIA

But r chats saved 2 hard drive 😵 😵 😵 😵 😵 ⌨️ 🖥️ 🖥️ 🖥️ 🖨️ 😮 😦 😐 😮 😵

PRIANKA

No clue 😵 😵

VICTORIA

U have like 3 days 2 figure this out 😫 😫 😬 👻 😮 😵 😈 😵 😵

CECILY

Um ok 💁 💁 💁

PRIANKA

Stay calm peeps 🕊️ 🕊️ ☮️ ☮️ ☮️ ☮️

OMG ORIGINAL  SQUAD

P C G

GABRIELLE

Guys, do u know what this means 😬 🙄 😮 😦 😦 😮

I took Vic off chat bc I am freaking out & don't want her mom to see 🙀 🙀 🙀

The bra pic is on comps omg 😲 😲 😲 😲

CECILY

I just texted it so delete text 😠 🙄 😬 😦

PRIANKA

I think they r still on their hard drive or whatevs or somehow IDK 👎 👎 👎

Who cares 💁 💁 💁 💁

Bras aren't illegal 😸 😆

GABRIELLE

Yeah but Jamal will c the pics 👀 👁 👓 🕶

PRIANKA

Its ok, Gabs

CECILY

We're not supposed to use comps for anything but school stuff 📚 📚 📚

PRIANKA

Hmmm IDK

Chill 4 now peeps 🐣 🐣 🐣 😎 😎

From: Diana Katz
To: Elizabeth Anderson, Manjula Basak, Cecily Anderson, Gabrielle Katz, Prianka Basak
Subject: Mamas and daughters day

Hi, dearies:

I think we found a date that works for everyone! Thursday is early dismissal for Take-a-Break Day of Spirit Week! We can all go out for ice cream and then go to Great Shapes!

Sound good? I hope so.

Love you all,
Diana

OMG YOUR MOM

CECILY

Gabbbbbs, ur mom 😅😂😆🙄😜

OMG 😲😐👽👻

GABRIELLE

I knowwwwww 😬🙄😬😮😐😲😮 😵

PRIANKA

LOL she is so funny 😆😆😆

This is NBD guys 💁💁💁💁

Maybe even fun 🎉🎉🎉

GABRIELLE

How r u guys

CECILY

Fine still working on this essay
⌨️💻🖥️🖨️

PRIANKA

I'm good

GABRIELLE

I am so annoyed about my mom & stressed about getting finals back 2morrow 😬 🙄
😬 😦 😨 😕 😮 😵

UGH 🥺 😩 🙀

TBH TOO MUCH DRAMA 4 last week of yr
😩 😩 😩 😩 😩 😩 😩 😩 😩 😩 😩 😩 😩

PRIANKA

It's ok, Gabs ☮️ ☮️ ☮️ 👍 😇 😴 😺

We luv u 😻 😻 😻 😻 😻

Arjun, Vishal, Prianka

ARJUN

R u guys going to bal vihar party

VISHAL

Yeah

PRIANKA

Same

VISHAL

Gonna be mad boring

PRIANKA

If we get bored we can make memes

How funny is this

CECE + PATCHES CUDDLING SINCE BIRTH

ARJUN

Hahahahahahaha

VISHAL

U made that?

PRIANKA

No Gabs did but it cracks me up

VISHAL

Super funny

ARJUN

Ha

I g2g bye

PRIANKA

Same c u guys tomorrow 👍

GOOD MORNING friendssssss

(P) (C) (G) (V)

VICTORIA

We r on way 2 school 🏫🎒🏫

Philly friends Kim & Nicole r w/ me woooo hooo 🎊🎉🎀🎈🎆🎇

CECILY

C u all soon

GABRIELLE

So nervous about getting finals back 😨😮
📖📕📓✏️

CECILY

Me 2

PRIANKA

Whatevs I am already in summer mode 😎
🕶️ 😎 👙 👙 👙 👙

GABRIELLE

LOL, Pri 🙄 😵

PRIANKA

 💁 💁 💁

ESSAY CONTEST

REFLECTIONS ON THE SCHOOL YEAR

by Cecily Anderson

Second draft

It has been an exciting year for me. I've enjoyed being sixth-grade rep. I think we've grown a great deal in terms of bullying and understanding one another. I think we still have a ways to go, though. Sometimes people are going through something and they don't feel comfortable sharing it or opening up to friends or teachers or family. ~~Maybe I can~~ Maybe there is a way to be aware of this and be on the lookout for it. So we can all help when we are struggling. I'm not sure how

GOOD MORNING friendsssssss

CECILY

Guys this essssssaaaaayyyy
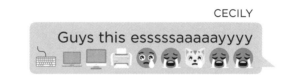

Think I'm gonna give up 👀😭😦

Not coming out how I want it to

GABRIELLE

Same

PRIANKA

Gabs, u should stick 2 memes LOL 😆😂
😁

GABRIELLE

Ew rude 🚫🙊🙊🙊

VICTORIA

LOL u guys

U r all funny 😂😂😂

ORIGINAL SQUAD

GABRIELLE

V's friends are so nice

Don't u think

CECILY

Yes def ✔ ✔

Where r u

We need 2 be @ singdown in 3 min

GABRIELLE

1st floor bathroom 🚽 🚽 🚽 🚽

PRIANKA

Ewww 😫 😫

GABRIELLE

Not peeing just texting LOL 😂 😂

PRIANKA

That's Gabs's official catchphrase 👍 👍

CECILY

LOL 😂 😂

Pri, where r u

PRIANKA

By lockers 🔐 🔒 🔓

No one is here

Where r u

CECILY

Comp lab 💻 ⌨️

Working on my essay

PRIANKA

Ooooh 🐱 🐱 🐱

GABRIELLE

Meeting u there, Cece

PRIANKA

Me 2 🏃🏃🏃

CECILY

555-55

YORKVILLE MIDDLE SCHOOL TEXT
ALERT: Attention, all students and parents:
Please join us after school for a community
service project. We are repainting the
fences around the courtyard! There will be
pizza! #SpiritWeek #YorkvilleUnited

Plans????

PRIANKA

Guyssss can't believe we were separated during singdown 💁🎤💁🎤💁🎤

I'm by lockers now & I don't see u 🔐🔒

R u all going 2 paint 🖌🖼🎨🖼🖌

Helloooooo

Bal Vihar Party

VISHAL

Want 2 carpool 4 bal vihar party l8r

PRIANKA

IDK maybe

ARJUN

I am going early 2 set up

VISHAL

Arj is now hardcore Bal Vihar participant

ARJUN

LOL I am

PRIANKA

Did u guys go 2 paint

IDK where my friends r

VISHAL

No I went home

ARJUN

Same

PRIANKA

Argh where r my friends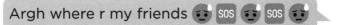

VISHAL

Boo hooo IDK

PRIANKA

Ew bye

CODE RED PRI DRAMA

P   C   G

PRIANKA

Guys where r u 4 real 🙀 SOS 🙀 SOS 🙀

I need 2 talk 2 u 😬 SOS 😬 SOS 😬

CECILY

We r painting 🖌️🖼️🎨🖼️🖌️🖌️🖼️🎨🖼️🖌️

Come

Sorry so late

Just saw ur messages

PRIANKA

K coming 🏃💨🏃💨🏃

76

CODE RED PRI DRAMA

P C G

PRIANKA

Every1 take a painting break `SOS` `SOS` `SOS`

GABRIELLE

Pri! We r here 2 work 👩‍💼 💼 👩‍💼 💼 👩‍💼 💼 🎨 🎨

PRIANKA

Need 2 talk 2 u guyssss ✋ 🙅

BTW Vic & pals r really into this

GABRIELLE

IK

PRIANKA

Where is Cece **❓ ❓ ❓**

GABRIELLE

By front fence

PRIANKA

Wahhhhh

Guyysssssss

Fine back 2 painting

At least there's 🍕 🍕 🍕 🍕 🍕 🍕

CODE RED PRI DRAMA

CECILY

Hi so sorry about b4

Didn't c texts

What's up?

Bad on finals? 😬 🙄 😬 🙄 😬 🙄

PRIANKA

No I did well 👍👍

U guys?

GABRIELLE

All As except for B+ in math and B+ in science 😎 😳 😐

CECILY

I did well 2

PRIANKA

🐰🎉🐰🎉🎉

CECILY

So how can we help

PRIANKA

Ummmm IDK if u can

GABRIELLE

Spill it, Pri

PRIANKA

Ummmmm

Cecily, Gabrielle

GABRIELLE

WIGO w/ her

CECILY

IDK

GABRIELLE

I know no side chats but...

CECILY

Let's c what she says

GABRIELLE

K

CODE RED PRI DRAMA

P C G

PRIANKA

Sooooooo

1st of all—we need 2 do more shared notebook 📓📓📓

CECILY

YES

What is 2nd of all?

PRIANKA

I don't think I like Vishal anymore 🚫💔🚫

GABRIELLE

WHAT WHY HOW ⁉️⁉️⁉️

CECILY

Yeah I am shocked 2 😵😵😵

PRIANKA

IDK he said 1 annoying thing

& now I just don't feel it anymore 🧖‍♀️

Is that how it works?

PRIANKA

I guess so

GABRIELLE

TBH IDK bc I still luv Colin LOL 😻😻😻😻

PRIANKA

LOL but 4 real 😹😹😹

CECILY

Yeah IDK either obvs

PRIANKA

What shud I do

GABRIELLE

Ummmmm 😬 🙀

Well school is over so soon sooooooo

PRIANKA

Just avoid ❓❓

CECILY

Just keep it chill

PRIANKA

IDK super stressed 😫 😫 😫

It just sorta happened that I don't like him like that anymore

CECILY

From 1 thing?

PRIANKA

Kinda yea

CECILY

I guess crushes come fast and go fast
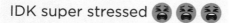

GABRIELLE

Exactly

GABRIELLE

It will b ok 👍👍👍

Good thing school's almost over 🏫🏫🎒
🏫🎒

CECILY

Srsly

Title of my essay should be TBH TOO
MUCH DRAMA

GABRIELLE

LOL 4 real 😂 😂 😂

PRIANKA

Haahahah

Totes thx guys

CECILY

ILY2SM

GABRIELLE

DITTO ☑ ☑

Guysssss so happy we are back with shared notebook! Why did we wait so long? Guess we got off track with finals but now we are BACK, BABIES! Okay—**first** order of biz—Pri and Vishal. IDK. **Second** order of biz—getting everything off our comps. And **third** order of biz—this bra shopping with moms. OMG too much to figure out. WTH?

Okay. I'm fine w/ bra shopping. It won't be that bad. FOR REAL. All girls wear a bra sooner or later, right!?!?

I think I will just be distant from Vishal and then it's summer anyway. It'll be okay. For this minute, I am kinda feeling calmer about it. More stressed about comps. I am going to casually ask my dad bc he does all that work with business and networks or whatever. IDEK what he does. LOL. Love u guys! Xoxox —PRI THE EXTRAORDINARY

SILVER GIRLS 4 LIFE

VICTORIA

Nic & Kim luv u guys so much 🐺🐺🐺🐺

CECILY

Awwwww

GABRIELLE

We r fab 🧜‍♀️🐰

PRIANKA

Obvs 👊👊👊👊

GABRIELLE

I love them too! ☑️

VICTORIA

Can u all come hang @ my house & have pizza 2night 🏡🍕

PRIANKA

I can after bal vihar party ☑️✔️☑️

Shouldn't be that long

CECILY

Ohh I can't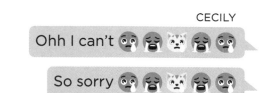

So sorry 😳😢🐱😩😳

PRIANKA

What r u doing, Cece

CECILY

Don't laugh ok 😳😁😆😁

GABRIELLE

Ummm underwater basket weaving?

CECILY

What??? LOL no

But I'm hanging w/ Mara b4 she leaves for camp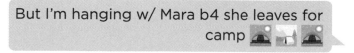

PRIANKA

Cece is an M girl LOL

CECILY

Stop

PRIANKA

U know I am JK

CECILY

IK

VICTORIA

Will miss u, Cece 😿 😿 😿

U guys like pepperoni or plain or pineapple or

GABRIELLE

LOL anything ok w/ me

PRIANKA

Same

Cecily, Mom

Hi, Mom, heading home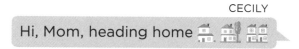

MOM

See you soon

Love you

From: Prianka Basak
To: Yorkville Middle School Tech Staff
Subject: Computers

Hello, Ms. Starr and the tech staff:

I want to make sure my computer is in perfect shape to hand back in on Friday. Is there a way to check that all files are removed from the hard drive? Thank you.

Sincerely,
Prianka Basak
Grade 6

From: Yorkville Middle School Tech Staff
To: Prianka Basak
Subject: RE: computers

Dear Prianka,

Don't worry about it. We have a system of removing all files before giving to a student next year.

Thanks for checking in. Have a great summer!

Ms. Starr

DOLPHIN SQUAD 🐬🐬🐬🐬

P C G

PRIANKA

Um guys

I'm so bored @ bal vihar party

I checked w/ Ms. Starr & she said they remove all files from comps when we turn them in ⌨️ 🖥️ 🖥️

GABRIELLE

But I don't want them or Jamal seeing r chats & bra pics 😬

CECILY

IK

PRIANKA

Think we can bring comps 2 Apple Store on r own

CECILY

IDK

I gtg

Prianka, Arjun

PRIANKA

Yo r u good @ using comps

ARJUN

??

Y r u texting me when we are 2gether

PRIANKA

Secret stuff

Can u make sure all stuff is off my comp b4 I return it

ARJUN

Ummm

No I don't think so

Ugh ok bye

Vic's NEW BFFs LOL

MAYBE: KIMBERLY

Hiiiii it's Kimberly 👩👩👩👩

Snuck on 2 vic's fone 2 get ur numbers 📲 📲 📲

Do u know her bday is on Fri 🎂 🎂 🎂 🎂

Since Nic + I r here we want to plan last min surprise party 🎉 🎉 🎉 🎉

MAYBE: NICOLE

Hiiii I'm (Nicole) here 2

94

Helloooo any1 there 👋🏻👋🏼👋🏻👋🏼

What do u guys think ⁉️⁉️⁉️

CECILY

Oooohhh 👏🏼👏🏼👏🏼👏🏼

GABRIELLE

Had no idea it was her bday soon 🎂🎂🎂🎂

MAYBE: NICOLE

IK she is weird about bdays

PRIANKA

OMG must plan this asap 🐰🐰💃🍴🏃

I am soooooooo in 🐰🐰🐰🐰🐰

MAYBE: KIMBERLY

Yesssssss but must be TOP SECRET 🙊🤐

CECILY

Of course ✔️☑️✔️

GABRIELLE

Obvs ✌️✌️✌️🤞

MAYBE: NICOLE

Can u help us fig out who else 2 invite
📩📩📩

PRIANKA

Yessss lets discuss @ pizza 🍕🍕🍕🍕

GABRIELLE

C u guyzzzz latersssss 😘😍🐺

OMGGGGGGGGGGGGGGGGGGGGGGGGG

(P)   (C)   (G)

GABRIELLE

Um guys 😲😐😟😣😨😧🙍

CECILY

What? 👂👂👂👂

PRIANKA

GABRIELLE

Somehow my meme went viral 🙈🙊

CECILY

The beans meme? 🔪🔪🔪

GABRIELLE

Noooo the Patches one

CECILY

What

How do u know 😋 👩 🙁

GABRIELLE

I went back 2 school bc I forgot my hoodie

Peeps were still there painting 🙁 🖌️ 👩 🎨 👨 🎨

& looking @ it 👀 🕵️ 🕵️ 🔭 🔭 🔍 🔍

I'm bugging out 😠 😵 😟 😲 😧 😳 😠

IDK how it got out 😠 😠 😠 😠 😠 😠 😠

I only sent 2 u guys 😱 😧 😥 😭 😳 😫 🙇

Where did Pri go ⁉️ ⁉️ ⁉️

CECILY

I guess busy @ Bal Vihar party 💁 💁 💁

Arjun, Vishal, Prianka

PRIANKA

Did u guys send any1 the Patches meme 🐱🐱🐱🐱🐱

ARJUN

No

VISHAL

I just sent 2 Colin & Jared

PRIANKA

WHYYYYYYYYYYY 😡😡😡😡😡

VISHAL

Cuz it was funny

PRIANKA

U can't just send something out w/o permission 😡😖😖😖😖

Gabs said it went viral 😂🤣😡😫😖😣😬🙄

I will ask Col and

Guys put phones away we r not supposed 2 be texting now

OMGGGGGGGGGGGGGGGGGGGGGGGG

(P) (C) (G)

CECILY

U guys I am so so so so so so so so so so mad @ u 😬👀😰😢😩😫😫😣😖🙁 🙁😐😟😥😰

Now every1 in knows  I sleep with a stuffed animal

GABRIELLE

So sorry, Cece 🙍🙍🙍🙍

I never expected any1 to c it 😳😓😳😠 🙀

PRIANKA

I am so sorry 😖 😒 😩 🙀

I sent to Vishal bc it was so funny & he sent it 2 someone and IDK how every1 saw it 😳 😦

But 4 real Cece it's NBD 👍 👍

Tons of peeps sleep with stuffed animals 🐶 🐶 🐶 🐶 🐶 🐶 🐶 🐰 🐰 🐰

CECILY

It is 2 me 😡 😫

GABRIELLE

It's kind of private, Pri 😩 😩 😩

PRIANKA

How private if she wrote it 4 her camping fact ❓ ❓

CECILY

I didn't want whole  2 know

Gtg bye

SILVER GIRLS 4 LIFE

VICTORIA

Omg that meme, Cece 😬 😮

So funny but r u ok 🙄 🙄 🙄

CECILY

I am not ok 👹 😈 😠

VICTORIA

I sleep w/ a stuffed animal too 🐰 🐰 🐰

So many people do 😀 😌 😁

No one cares 4 real 👇 👇

PRIANKA

That's what I said, Vic 👍👍

NBD right ⁉️

VICTORIA

Totes NBD 🙌👏

GABRIELLE

I disagree 🤘🤘

PRIANKA

Then y did u make a meme of it, Gabsssssss 🙀😠😡😵

UGH BYE 👎👎

Cecily, Mara

C M

MARA

Running 10 min late 🏃🏃🏃💨

B there soon

CECILY

K no prob

I have s'mores stuff ready & my mom lit the outdoor fire pit 🔥 ✴️ 🎆

MARA

So fab

Sorry about the meme thing

CECILY

UGH thnx 😖 😫 😣

MARA

We can discuss

K 🐱🐱🐱

DOLPHIN SQUAD MISSING CECE

(P) (C) (G)

GABRIELLE

So much fun @ pizza w/ Vic, Nic & Kim 🍕
🍕

We r so lucky we live so close 2 Jennie's 🍕
🍕 🍕 🍕

But we miss u, Cece 😳 😩 🐱

PRIANKA

Miss u soooooo much 😳 😳 😳 😳

Even tho u r so mad @ me 😫 😫 😫 😫 😫

GABRIELLE

How's neighbor BFF time w/ Mara 👭 👭 👭 👭

Cece????

PRIANKA

Earth to Cece 🌍 🌏 🌎

Come in, Cece

DOLPHIN SQUAD MISSING CECE

CECILY

Hi, guys

I didn't look @ my phone until now
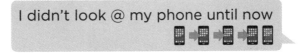

GABRIELLE

So much fun w/ Mara?

CECILY

Yes

She made me feel better about the meme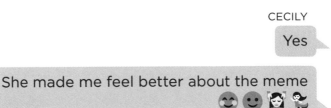

But I'm still kinda mad, Pri 😾😾😾😾

PRIANKA

I am so sorry 😣

I didn't expect so many peeps 2 c it 😫 🙄

Just sent to Vishal and Arj 4 real

Did Mara think it was NBD

CECILY

She could c both sides of it 😦 😦 😼

PRIANKA

Ok 😥

BTW we made more plans 4 V's bday 🎂
🎂 🎂 🎂

Will fill u in tomw

CECILY

K night

GABRIELLE

Smooches 💋 💋 💋 💋

Cecily, Mara

Thx for listening to me blabber on about the meme 😣 😢 ☹️

MARA

No prob

Hope I helped u

CECILY

U did

MARA

Don't stress 4 real 💆 💆 💆 💆

People forget everything super fast 👍 👍

& who cares anyway 🙏 🙏

CECILY

Yea I guess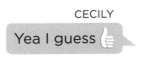

109

Thanks gnight

Dear Diary,

So the whole school knows I sleep with a stuffed animal. Gabs made a meme and Pri sent it to Vishal and he sent it to Colin and blah blah. Too annoying to write about. So embarrassing.

Mara just left. It's official. I have a crush on her. I was so sad when she had to go. And we had so much fun. I didn't look at my phone even one time! It doesn't feel like a regular friendship. Like with Pri and Gabs obviously I love them. But this feels different. I just want to be with her all the time. When we hugged at the end, I waited until she pulled away first. Is that so weird? I don't know how this happened.

Love,
Cecily

V'S PARTAAAYYYYYYY

(P) (C) (G) (K) (N)

NICOLE

Thx so much for ur help 💃🏼💃🏼💃🏼🧜🏻‍♀️🕺

Sooooooo happy we can have it in ur backyard, Pri 🌳🌳🌲🌳

PRIANKA

NP 😃😊😃😊

Happy 2 help 😊😎😎

CECILY

Who is coming from school? 🏫🎒🏫🎒

PRIANKA

IDK 👩🏻👩🏻👩🏻👩🏻

Gabs was in charge of invites

111

GABRIELLE

I just told peeps 2 spread the word since so last min and IDK who will be free 👩📱👨
📱👩👩👧👦👩👩🏃🏃🏃👯👯

PRIANKA

So basically whole grade could come??!?!
😂😂😂😂😂😂😂😂

GABRIELLE

U have a huge backyard, Pri
🌲🌲🌳🌲🌳

PRIANKA

IK but still 😂😂😂😂😂😂😂😂😨😲
😨😵😵😾🙀

Who is buying food 🍕🍕🍕🥞🧇🥓🍞
🍔🌭🍟🍭🍦🍪🍩🥠🍥

NICOLE

We r

V's mom gave us a gift card 2 order 🍕🍕
🍕 & she's having soda and chips delivered

PRIANKA

Um ok 😎👍🙌

If Cece wins essay contest she could pay
for all of the 🍕🍕🍕 LOL

NICOLE

LOL 😹😹😹😹

PRIANKA

Need 2 tell my rents 👩👨

I gtg bye mwah

KIMBERLY

Is she mad @ us 😿😓😨

CECILY

No don't worry 💁💁💁💁💁💁

GABRIELLE

NO she said mwah 💋😽😽😘

YORKVILLE MIDDLE SCHOOL TEXT ALERT: Good morning! Come to the lobby as soon as you get to school. Bagels for everyone! #HappySpiritWeek #YorkvilleUnited

BRA SHOPPING DAY

(P) (C) (G)

PRIANKA

Omg u guys

Bra shopping 2day 4 real

GABRIELLE

IK ugh 😟 😢 ☹️ ☹️ ☹️ 😖

What a week

CECILY

Srsly crazy week ♉ 〰️ 😜 😳 😊 😝

114

Still think it's weird that u think the stuffed animal thing is NBD 😭 😢 😦 😬 🙀 🙀

GABRIELLE

I'm w/ u on this 1, Cece 😫 😫 😫

PRIANKA

It's how I feel but I get how u guys feel 2 😢 🙁 🙁 🙍 🙍

CECILY

Pri, whatevs, we have to put this debate on hold anyway since we have more awk stuff going on 😲 😜 😂 😁 😈 😈 👹 👺 🤡 🙍 🙍 🤡 🙍

Hello bra shopping uggghhh 👙 👙 👙

Notice no bra emoji 🙄 🙄

PRIANKA

Wahhhhhh x 2 🙄 🙄 🙄 🙄 😵 😵

At least it's a short day @ school 👍 👍

Bagels & then teams go off for comm serv projects right? 🥯👩🍳👨🍳🍽️🍴

No bagel emoji either 🙄 🙄

yes 2 the schedule 👈 👈

Blue team is singing @ nursing home 🎵🎶🎤

We r cleaning up trash by beach and library 🗑️🗑️🏖️🏝️

IDK what we r doing 🤔

I forgot 🤔 🤔 🤔 🙄

Ohhhhh we r making sandwiches @ food pantry 🍔🍔🍔🍔🍔

Then we all meet back @ school @ 12:30 & we r freeeeee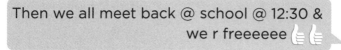

PRIANKA

Free 2 get boob support 😹😹

GABRIELLE

LOL, PRI 😹😹😹😹😹😹😹😹😹

PRIANKA

It's NBD

Let's chill about boob support 😊😍😘😺😼

U think everything is NBD, Pri 😡😡😡😡

PRIANKA

Not true 😣😣😣😣😣

From: Prianka Basak
To: Cecily Anderson, Gabrielle Katz, Victoria Melford
Subject: FWD: Erasing data from computer

Guysssssss—

See what guy from Apple Store said. We need to go later today w/o our moms knowing!

> **From:** Trevor
> **To:** Prianka Basak
> **Subject:** RE: Erasing data from computer
>
> Dear Prianka:
>
> Thanks for inquiring. It's not usually a problem to wipe a computer of its data. Make sure you have everything you need backed up! Stop in when you can. Best to have a parent with you.
>
> Peace,
> Trevor @ Yorkville Apple Store

Guys, moving this discussion to notebook since
we don't want to put anything else on computers
before we turn in. Must go back to old-fashioned
ways. LOL

Oh good idea! Have 1 sec to write this since we
are parting ways for community service projects.
Byeeeeeee

Same same. Mwah! xoxo

ESSAY CONTEST

REFLECTIONS ON THE SCHOOL YEAR

by Cecily Anderson

Third draft

Reflecting on the school year is hard since we still technically have a couple days left. Anything can happen. More and more I am realizing that things can change in an instant: feelings, friendships, struggles, hardships, achievements. Basically, anything can change at any time. It's so scary to realize that, but also so exciting. It basically means that we can't get too bogged down with one thing for too long because we know it will change. And we can't expect that good times will last forever, either, because they'll change, too. There's comfort in knowing that so many things are temporary. Sometimes secrets are revealed and you realize that certain things are meant to stay private and it's okay for other things to come out. And you never know how you feel until the time comes.

I may have made some progress on the essay, guys. We'll discuss at BRA SHOPPING. LOL. Do we all go into the fitting room together? I mean, what is going to happen exactly? Why does this feel so confusing? I should've asked Ingrid about her bra shopping experience. Oh well.

From: Steven Macdonald
To: Edward Carransey
Subject: Phenomenal job

Dear Ed,

The students from Yorkville were phenomenal today. All of them were enthusiastic and kind to the residents at the retirement community. This was the best group we've ever had. Keep doing what you're doing! The world is becoming a happier, more cheerful place.

A million thanks to you and the Yorkville Middle School students!

All best,
Steve

Steven Macdonald
Executive Director
Yorkville Springs Retirement Community

BOOB DRAMA

P   C   G

GABRIELLE

OMG this is insane 😼😼😼😼😼

I'm so sorry guys 🙀😾🙀😾🫤

PRIANKA

Why r u sorry ☹️☹️☹️

GABRIELLE

Soooooo embarrassing 😬😬😬😬

My mom dragged u all in2 it 😔

OMG the way they have 2 measure us
📏📏📏📏📏📏

Who r these ladies ⁉️⁉️⁉️⁉️⁉️⁉️

So awk 🙀🙀

PRIANKA

LOL it is awk but its ok 👍👍👍

CECILY

Srsly I am happy w/ my sports bra TBH

GABRIELLE

& TBH way way way 2 much drama for last week of school 😂😂😂😂

Oh lord here's the lady w/ more bras 4 us

PRIANKA

Omggggg stoppppp ✋🖐

Why do we need this many choices 🙅‍♀️🙆‍♀️🙇‍♀️🏃‍♀️

CECILY

I think r moms r enjoying this 2 much LOL 😆😆😆😆😆😆😆😆😆

GABRIELLE

Haha they just glared at us 2 stop texting 📱📲📴📳🔋

PRIANKA

This is kinda funny, guys 😂 😂 😂 😂

GABRIELLE

Thank gd u r here w/ me tho 🐰 🐰 🐰 🐰

4 real 🐰 🙌 🙌

CECILY

Ughhh here I go back 2 the dressing room 😔 😧 😦 😠 😵 😵 😖

GABRIELLE

UGH LOL 😵 😭 😂 😄 😂 😁

125

Reflections on bra shopping with friends and moms:

First of all, I think this would have been way worse without you guys. But second of all, even though it was kind of bad, we made it through. I think bra shopping is one of those things you just kinda do and pray it ends fast. What do you guys think?
Xox Pri the Extraordinary

Ummmm, yeah, I agree. Maybe it's best to shop for bras online? Those ladies were mega intense.

TOTALLY! All up in our biz, people!! NO THANK YOU. Sorry my mom made us do this. Luv, Gabs

R we all set 4 Apple Store after this?

Yes, it's only 2 blocks away—will tell moms we need 2 check something 4 school.

Yea, and they will want coffee anyway or tea or scones or whatever moms like.

TOO MUCH DRAMA 🎭🎭🎭🎭

P C G

CECILY

CECILY

Switching 2 text bc moms were trying 2 snoop @ notebook 📓📔📘

PRIANKA

They snoop @ everything duh 👀🙄👀🙄🙄🙄🙄

GABRIELLE

True 😳😭😹😼😹😼😼

CECILY

K they r paying 4 bras 💳💳💳💳

We say we need 2 check something @ Apple Store 4 seventh grade 💻💻💻📱📔📔📔📔📔📚📖

PRIANKA

Got it 👍

128

What do we say when we get 2 🍎

GABRIELLE

??

CECILY

That we want 2 make sure all data is off comps 🖥️ 🖥️

PRIANKA

TBH peeps @ school won't know when we used iMessage 📧

It's ok to iMessage on school comps @ nite @ home? 🏡🏫🏡

GABRIELLE

IDK 👧 👧

CECILY

Either way its better if stuff is off of comps 👍👍👍

GABRIELLE

K true 😳 😳 😳

PRIANKA

K, Cece, u lead the way 🏃🏃🏃🏃

OMG y me 👻 😐 😵 😮

PRIANKA

Bc u know whats going on 😂 😁 😂

Ur r fearless leader 💪 💪 💪 💪 😊 😊

GABRIELLE

LOL but it's true, Cece 😂 😂 😂 😂 😂

CECILY

Um ok 😦 🙁 🙃 😏

Gabrielle, Mom

MOM

Gabs, there's a bit of a wait @ Coffee Klatch so all of you meet us back here when you're done at the Apple 🍎 Store

GABRIELLE

Ok 😘😘

BFF POWER SQUAD

P C G

GABRIELLE

Guys, we have a bit more time ⏰ ⏱️ ⧖ ⧗

Moms r not meeting us @ 🍎 anymore

PRIANKA

K

CECILY

K

BFF POWER SQUAD

GABRIELLE

What is Apple Store dude talking about 🙄
🙄😖😞⁉️

PRIANKA

IDK but we can't text & talk to him 🤦🏽‍♀️

So rude

GABRIELLE

But I am so confused & scared to ask 😀
😥😲😡😳😐🙁😖😩😫

Cece, u handle & we will walk away for a
min 🙈🙈🙈

CECILY

Ummm IDK y but ok 🤦🏽‍♀️🤦🏽‍♀️

BFF POWER SQUAD

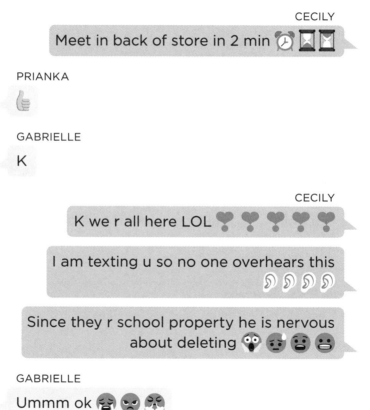

CECILY

Meet in back of store in 2 min ⏰⌛⌛

PRIANKA

👍

GABRIELLE

K

CECILY

K we r all here LOL 💛💛💛💛💛

I am texting u so no one overhears this 👂👂👂👂

Since they r school property he is nervous about deleting 😱😥😨😬

GABRIELLE

Ummm ok 😪😠🙀

PRIANKA

What should we do

CECILY

I don't think there is anything we can do 😵😭😵😭😭

PRIANKA

Ummmmm 😫😤😠😤

GABRIELLE

Freaking out 😨 😵 😮

We sent each other memes & stuff

& look what happened 😵 😵 😵

& Jamal seeing bra pics OMG 😵 😵 😵 😵 😵 😵 😵 😵 😵

PRIANKA

IK !!!!!!!

135

Ummmm ✌️☝️

Maybe we just go talk to Mr. C & Mr. A & explain and say we r sorry & own it ✌️

That sounds way scary, Cece 😮 😮 😦 😧 😮

IK but IDK what 2 do 🙇 🙇 🙇

We gtg meet moms

Continue discussing 2night

K 🙁 🙁 🙁

What a day guys 😫 😫

IK 4 real 🙀 😿 😿 😓

PARTY FOR V!!!!

NICOLE

U guys all set 4 the party 🎀🎏🎊🎈🎁

Any idea how many peeps r coming

PRIANKA

No clue really

But all good bc I can fit whole grade in my backyard 🌳🌴🌱🌿☘️🍀🍃🎋🍁🌾

GABRIELLE

We r happy to include every1 ✌️✌️✌️✌️

CECILY

Totally 💪💪💪💪

PRIANKA

Cece are Mara + M girls coming 👯👯👯
💃

I think so

GABRIELLE

We r not jealous that u luv Mara 😂 😂 😂

LOL 😂 😂 😂 😂 😂

CECILY

No reason 2 b 👍 🙂 😀

I gg finish end of year essay ✏️ 🖊️ 🖋️ 📝 📖

NICOLE

Good luck 🍀 🍀 🍀 🍀

KIMBERLY

C u guys tomw

Vishal, Prianka

VISHAL

Yo

PRIANKA

Yo

VISHAL

R u ok

PRIANKA

Yeah why

VISHAL

I feel like things r weird

PRIANKA

No

VISHAL

No I mean I feel that way

PRIANKA

Ok

VISHAL

See u r being weird now

PRIANKA

I'm sorry, Vishal

VISHAL

Bout what

PRIANKA

IDK

VISHAL

???

PRIANKA

I think we r better as friends

VISHAL

Um

Is this bc of the meme

PRIANKA

Kinda but I felt that way b4

C u tomw

VISHAL

K bye

EMERGENCY TEXT SESH

P C G

PRIANKA

Hello !??!??

Need u guys SOS SOS SOS SOS SOS

CECILY

What's up 😳😨

PRIANKA

I told Vishal we r better as friends 😨😳😱

GABRIELLE

Ok that's good 🙆🙆

PRIANKA

I feel bad 🥺😩🙀

GABRIELLE

It's how u feel 🌠⭐⭐✨⚡☄️💥🔥🌪️🌈☀️

CECILY

Always need 2 b true 2 how u feel 👆👈👊

TBH DUH 😹😹😹😹

PRIANKA

IK 😕😖😣😢

But how did feelings change so fast 💔💔

GABRIELLE

IDK 🤦‍♀️🤦‍♀️

CECILY

I think it's just the way it works 😍😘😻

Ingrid is always in love w/ someone new 😍😘😻💌❤️❤️❤️❤️💕💞💜

+ she's way older than us 🙇‍♀️🙇‍♀️🙇‍♀️

PRIANKA

Yeah 🙈🙈

Gabs, do u still like Col 👦❓

143

GABRIELLE

IDK kinda 🖤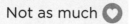

Not as much 🤍

PRIANKA

Cece, any changes 4 you ❓❓

CECILY

Not really IDK 🙅‍♀️

PRIANKA

Vic still 💚 Arjun rite?

GABRIELLE

I think so 😎😍

PRIANKA

Well my luv 4 u guys will never change 💕
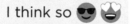

GABRIELLE

100% 4 ever 😻😻😻

CECILY

Samey samey 💜💜💜💜💜

So excited 4 camping trip

1 more week

PRIANKA

YES DEF DEF DEF 👏👏👏

CECILY

Guys, I'm going 2 email tech dept again &
ask if we can meet w/ them ☮️☮️☮️☮️

Vic has nothing on her ⌨️🖥️🖥️ rite?

GABRIELLE

No bc she got in so much trouble she
never brought it home and she never even
opened iMessage again 📓📓📘📕

PRIANKA

Oy ok she's safe 👌👌👌

145

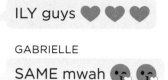

ILY guys 🖤🖤🖤

GABRIELLE

SAME mwah 😘 😘

From: Cecily Anderson
To: Yorkville Middle School Tech Staff
Subject: computer question

Hello, Ms. Starr, and everyone on the tech staff:

Is it possible for Gabrielle Katz, Prianka Basak, and me to stop in and talk to you tomorrow morning?

Please let me know. Thank you.

Sincerely,
Cecily Anderson

I'm not afraid of storms, for I'm learning how to sail my ship. —Louisa May Alcott

146

REFLECTIONS ON THE SCHOOL YEAR

by Cecily Anderson

Millionth draft (I've lost count)

I'm going to reflect on why this essay is so hard for me to write. It's hard to sum up a whole year in a short essay. Sometimes I feel like each day lasts for a hundred years. And other times I feel like the weeks fly by. I'm not sure why that is. I think it's because things are changing so fast. I've been pushing that feeling aside because I really do want to stay a kid for as long as possible. I like being a kid. I like not having to think about that many important, scary things. I like playing outside and riding bikes with my friends and even playing with dolls sometimes, too. I don't need to be embarrassed that I still sleep with a stuffed animal. It's who I am. I need to be truthful about myself and all things.

From: Yorkville Middle School Tech Staff
To: Cecily Anderson
Subject: RE: computer question

Hello, Cecily:

Sure. Please stop in tomorrow before the charades competition! We will all be in the office.

Ms. Starr

BEST SQUAD IN THE WORLD

P C G

CECILY

Do u guys think the winning essay will be
published

I am kinda writing private stuff 😕 😬 🙄

PRIANKA

IDK

Ask Mr. C

GABRIELLE

Yeah 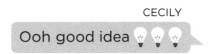 him

CECILY

Ooh good idea 💡 💡 💡

149

From: Cecily Anderson
To: Edward Carransey
Subject: quick question

Dear Mr. C,

Will the winning essay contest essay be published or posted somewhere? Not that I think I will win or anything but I'm just curious. I am writing some personal things.

Thank you,
Cecily Anderson

I'm not afraid of storms, for I'm learning how to sail my ship. —Louisa May Alcott

ESSAY CONTEST

REFLECTIONS ON THE SCHOOL YEAR

by Cecily Anderson

Millionth draft (I've lost count)

I'm going to reflect on why this essay is so hard for me to write. It's hard to sum up a whole year in a short essay. Sometimes I feel like each day lasts for a hundred years. And other times I feel like the weeks fly by. I'm not sure why that is. I think it's because things are changing so fast. I've been pushing that feeling aside because I really do want to stay a kid for as long as possible. I like being a kid. I like not having to think about that many important, scary things. I like playing outside and riding bikes with my friends and even playing with dolls sometimes, too.

I think sixth grade was basically a year of huge change and growth and that made it hard. Looking back on it now, it feels like a major year. But as I was going through it, it just felt hard.

Maybe we don't know what things really are until they're over. Although we still have one more day.

From: Edward Carransey
To: Cecily Anderson
Subject: RE: quick question

Hi, Cecily,

We are not sure yet if the winning essay will be published. Perhaps we will leave it up to the winner. To be determined. Good luck! Happy writing!

All the best,
Mr. C

*Be the change you want to see in the world.
—Gandhi*

From: Cecily Anderson
To: Gabrielle Katz, Prianka Basak
Subject: FWD: re: quick question

Guys, see below. Are we all okay with this?

Xoxo Cecily

> **From:** Yorkville Middle School Tech Staff
> **To:** Cecily Anderson
> **Subject:** RE: computer question
>
> Hello, Cecily:
>
> Sure. Please stop in tomorrow before the charades competition! We will all be in the office.
>
> Ms. Starr

BEST SQUAD IN THE WORLD

P C G

PRIANKA

I'm ok w/ Ms. Starr meeting ✓ ✓ ✓ ✓

I didn't want to reply on email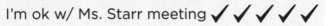

CECILY

K cool ☑ ☑

GABRIELLE

I'm ok w/ it 2 ✓ ✓

We r just gonna be all TBH THERE
HAS BEEN SO MUCH DRAMA WITH
COMPUTERS PLEASE HELP US AHHHHH
🔥 🔥 🔥 🔥 🔥 🔥

PRIANKA

LOL 😂 😁

CECILY

Kinda that sounds like a good plan LOL
😂 😁 😂 😁

Cecily, Mara

C M

CECILY

R u going to the surprise 🎊 🎉 4 Victoria

MARA

Yeah

It's @ Prianka's 🏠🏡🏘️🏡🏠 rite

CECILY

Yeah

R ur friends going 2 ✨✨✨✨

MARA

IDK

CECILY

K well c u soon 👋👋👋👋

MARA

K bye 👋👋👋

555-55

YORKVILLE MIDDLE SCHOOL TEXT ALERT: Reminder to all students that all school laptops must be returned by three p.m. today. Have a wonderful summer!

BFFFFFFFFFFFFFFFFFFFFFFFFF

(P) (C) (G)

PRIANKA

Guys r we all ready for Ms. Starr meeting

GABRIELLE

 but yea

CECILY

Same

PRIANKA

Honesty is best policy 🌈⭐🌈⭐🌍🌍 🌍🌠

Cheesy but true 🧀🧀🧀🧀

Hope day goes fast so we get 2 Vic's party 😆🎉🎊🎉🎊🎉🎊

GABRIELLE

Same so pumped 👏👏👏

Also gonna tell Col I just want 2 b friends 😐😬

PRIANKA

LOL we r all anti the boys now 🙈🙈🙈🙈

GABRIELLE

Haha I guess 😆😆😆

PRIANKA

Cece we r all over boy craziness 🤔🤔🤔

CECILY

LOL 😂😂

K time 4 meeting 🤝🤝🤝

Stay strong BFFs 💪💪💪

GABRIELLE

On it 💪 ⭐ 🤴 🤖 ⚡ 💥 🌪 🌬

PRIANKA

Yup ↔ ON! ↔ ON! ↔ ON!

CECILY

I 💜 💜 💜 💜 💝 🌍 💓 💚 you guysssssssss

From: Yorkville Middle School Tech Staff
To: Cecily Anderson, Prianka Basak, Gabrielle Katz
Subject: End of year computer turn-in follow-up

Hello, Cecily, Prianka, and Gabrielle:

The tech department and I are glad you stopped in today to discuss the state of your computers. First of all, it's always best to be honest up-front. This applies to life and technology. So, good job with that.

Jamal was busy with other duties so was not responsible for wiping your computers.

The tech teachers and I will take care of making sure everything is off the computers. It doesn't seem that there is anything too damaging. Please remember for next year—the computers are ONLY to be used for schoolwork. Do not even use them for iMessaging at night. As long as you keep it academic, you are OK. We will review this policy again in September.

Have a great summer.

Ms. Starr

PHEW

PRIANKA

Good idea 2 talk to Ms. Starr 💡💡💡

GABRIELLE

Agree 💥⚡💥

CECILY

We just have 2 be so careful next year ☮️✌️

Kinda glad school comps r turned in ⌨️💻🖥️🖨️🖱️🕹️

GABRIELLE

Same 👧🙍

Really glad this year is over 🌪️🔥💥☄️🌪️🌈☀️🌊

PRIANKA

Imagine if we just never texted again & only did shared notebook

160

How v

PRIANKA

No idea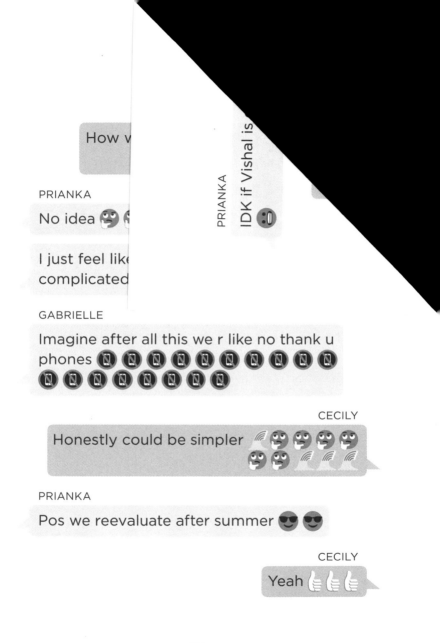

I just feel lik
complicated

IDK if Vishal is

PRIANKA

GABRIELLE

Imagine after all this we r like no thank u
phones 🔲🔲🔲🔲🔲🔲🔲🔲🔲🔲
🔲🔲🔲🔲🔲🔲🔲🔲

CECILY

Honestly could be simpler

PRIANKA

Pos we reevaluate after summer 😎😎

CECILY

Yeah 👍👍👍

coming 2 Vic's party 😬 😬

I feel like all boy craziness ended kinda suddenly 🚥 🚦 🚈 ⏱️

GABRIELLE

Yeah ur right ⏱️ 🏃 〰️ 🏃 ➡️

PRIANKA

Who knows 💥 💥 💥 💥 💥 💥

I am soooo ready 4 summer 😎 😎 ⛱️ ☀️

CECILY

Me 2 🕶️ 🕶️ 🕶️ 🕶️

Gtg finish essay 📖 ✏️ 🖊️ 📝

TTYL 👋 👋 👋

Mwah 💋 😘 💋 😻 😽

162

ESSAY CONTEST

REFLECTIONS ON THE SCHOOL YEAR

by Cecily Anderson

Gazillionth draft (I've lost count)

I'm going to reflect on why this essay is so hard
for me to write. It's hard to sum up a whole year
in a short essay. Sometimes I feel like each day
lasts for a hundred years. And other times I feel
like the weeks fly by. I'm not sure why that is. I
think it's because things are changing so fast. I've
been pushing that feeling aside because I really
do want to stay a kid for as long as possible. I like
being a kid. I like not having to think about that
many important, scary things. I like playing outside
and riding bikes with my friends and even playing
with dolls sometimes, too.

I think sixth grade was basically a year of huge
change and growth and that made it hard. Looking

back on it now, it feels like a major year. But as I was going through it, it just felt hard.

Maybe we don't know what things really are until they're over. I think the best advice I could give to someone about to enter middle school is to try and stay calm and not get stressed every time something changes or something new happens.

Another thing I learned this year is that there's only one way to go about life—and that way is to be yourself. Trying to be something that you're not honestly makes no sense and is actually kind of impossible. You just won't feel right. I mean, actors do it and that's cool but unless you're a professional actor, you need to be yourself to feel comfortable in this world. It's the only way.

This year was also monumental because it helped us all realize that feelings can be hurt completely accidentally. Yorkville is a kind place and I don't know many people here who go out of their way to hurt someone else. But it happens. I think we are all more aware now of our how actions impact others.

All in all, sixth grade was challenging and enlightening. I don't think I'm the same as I was on the first day of school.

I'm looking forward to a restful, peaceful summer, and I hope that we can all come back to Yorkville Middle School in September feeling refreshed and rejuvenated.

CHARADES 4 LIFE

PRIANKA

OMG u guys we crushed charades 👏 👏 👏

Sorry 2 brag but 4 real 👍 👍 👍 🖤 🖤 🖤

Did u see how great Sanda & I did 💃 👯 💃 👯

CECILY

Yessssss u were soooo good 👏 👏 👏

PRIANKA

Can we do charades @ the party 2nite 🎉 🎊 🎉 🎊 🎉 🎊

I am really feeling it 💃 💃 💃

NICOLE

LOL ok 😁 😂 😁

GABRIELLE

OMG I was soooo bad

I had no idea what Colin was doing

Haha LOL 😂 😂

It was hard 2 tell he was playing hockey 🏒🏒🏒🏒🏒🏒🏒🏒🏒

PRIANKA

IK he looked like he was whacking bugs 🐛
🐞 🦓 🐞

KIMBERLY

LOL this school is sooo funny 👹 👺 🤡 👻
💩 💀

We don't have this much fun in Phil

Good thing Vic moved here

PRIANKA

OMG I almost put Vic on this text & ruined
surprise 😨 😲 😦 😲

NICOLE

ACK thank the lord u didn't 🙌 🙌 🙌 🙏

167

PRIANKA

K see u peeps later

Come any time u want 2 set up

My parents r so happy every1 is getting along they don't care how many people come ☮ ☮ ☮ ☮

CECILY

Love that, Pri 💕 💞 🖤 🤍

GABRIELLE

Me 2 🤟

Cecily, Mara

C M

MARA

U want me 2 pick u up on the way to Prianka's?

CECILY

Sure that would be fab 😎 😎

My mom can drive us home

MARA

Cool

Dear Diary,

I am bugging out right now. I am going to see Mara at this party for Victoria in a few hours and I feel like I need to tell her how I feel. But the question is—do I tell her in person? Write her a letter? Send her a text?

I just need her to know before we are apart for the whole summer. I wonder if we can still be friends even if she doesn't like me like that. I mean, I doubt she does. I know she just thinks I'm a good friend. But I need to tell her anyway.

I have been debating telling Pri and Gabs about this since they love me and accept me no matter what. But I still feel weird about it. Am I the first girl at Yorkville Middle to have a crush on another girl? I have no idea.

xoxo

Cecily

Cecily, Prianka

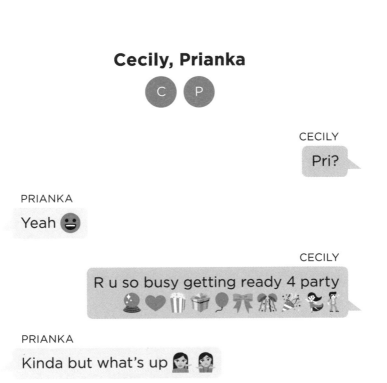

CECILY

Pri?

PRIANKA

Yeah 😀

CECILY

R u so busy getting ready 4 party 🔮❤️🍿🎁🎈🎀🎉🎆🧜‍♀️🧜

PRIANKA

Kinda but what's up 👧👩

CECILY

U know how we have been BFF since b4 we were born 👯👯👯👯👯

PRIANKA

Haha yes 👯👭

I kind of have a big secret & I want to tell some1 but I am scared

PRIANKA

Ummmm u know I love secrets 🤫

CECILY

IK & TBH the meme thing still annoys me but ur my BFF 4evs & I need 2 talk 2 u

PRIANKA

Ok....

TBH I'm worried bc ur not using emojis rn
😥 😲 😨 😳

CECILY

No I'm ok

PRIANKA

If ur not ready to tell it's NBD

CECILY

Yeah

PRIANKA

U r scared 2 tell Gabs?????

U know we said no side chats

CECILY

IK

PRIANKA

U know I am always here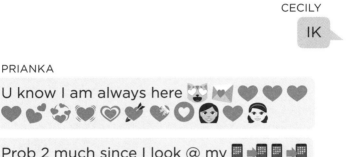

Prob 2 much since I look @ my every second

CECILY

LOL

Thx, Pri

Cecily, Gabrielle

GABRIELLE

Cece? 🤩 🫢 😍 🫢

CECILY

Yeah?

GABRIELLE

I just wanted 2 say sorry again 🙀 🫣 😣 😔 😕 😕 😕

4 making that meme

I didn't mean 4 it 2 go viral 😣 🙀 😣 🥺

& now I am kind of freaking out bc what if something else goes viral 😱

CECILY

Just b careful what u send & 2 who 👌 👌

Hope Pri learns that 2 but maybe it was kinda NBD 💁 💁 💁

GABRIELLE

Yeah I guess

I just feel bad 🐱😿😿

CECILY

IK

I gtg but ILY 💕💞💓💗

GABRIELLE

Same 💗💗💗

Cecily, Mara

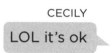

MARA

Sorry my mom talks so much

CECILY

LOL it's ok

MARA

Srsly she doesn't stop

CECILY

All moms talk a lot

MARA

Y tho

CECILY

IDK they have a lot 2 say

MARA

IDK I guess

It doesn't bother me

So don't worry k?

K

Happy we r going 2 the party 2gether

R Marissa & Mae coming

IDK they r weird lately

Really? U never said anything

IK it's awk

I'm glad u and me have become closer

CECILY

Same def

Can we talk @ party

MARA

Obv we can talk

What do u mean

CECILY

Like privately about something

MARA

Ummm now I'm nervous but ok

CECILY

Don't be nervous

I promise

MARA

K

PARTY PARTY PARTY

P C G V

PRIANKA

Guys every1 is having fun right 🐧🐰🕺🐰

GABRIELLE

Totally 👍👍

VICTORIA

Um yesssssss I can't believe u guys planned this 4 me 😳😊😬😄

PRIANKA

Vic, u & Arjun r sooooooo cute 2gether btw 💏💏💏

VICTORIA

IK 💓🤍💘💘💘🤍

PRIANKA

U have to really thank Kim & Nic 4 party tho 🎊🎉🎈🎁

VICTORIA

IK but Pri, ur hosting so thx 2 u
tooooooooooo 🎇🎇🎇🎇🎇

Sooooo nice 😻😻😻😻

PRIANKA

NP

This is so fun 🧜‍♀️🎪🤹‍♀️🎉🤡😺

Ok if I make an announcement? 📣📣📣
📣📣

I think it wd be fun if everyone wrote
anonymous wishes 4 summer 🌈🙇‍♀️🙇‍♀️🙏

& I put them all in a bowl 🍜

& then people reached in & pulled 1 out 🤛
👋✋

GABRIELLE

LOL, Pri 🙈

180

That feels so school-ish 🏫🎒🏫🎒🚫🚫🚫

VICTORIA

I like the idea 💡💡💡

DO IT 🛐🛐

PRIANKA

K whatev Vic wants LOL 🙌🙌🙌🙏

GABRIELLE

K true 👠👠👠

PRIANKA

Where is Cece ❓❓❓

GABRIELLE

I saw her b4 on the hammock w/ Mara in some serious conv 💆💆💆

PRIANKA

K they r so serious 🤪🤪🤪

181

VICTORIA

Haha they really are 🕶️ 🕶️

PRIANKA

Sorry we r texting about u Cece 😘 😘

Back 2 party 🎊 🎉 🎈 🎊 🎉 🎈

Bye 🐱

Vishal, Prianka

VISHAL

Can we talk

PRIANKA

Sure

VISHAL

Where r u

PRIANKA

Lol Vishal I see u texting me

I am by soda duh

VISHAL

K

PARTY PARTY PARTY

P C G V

PRIANKA

1 more thing

Vish wants 2 talk now

So if u wonder where I am....

555-55

YORKVILLE MIDDLE SCHOOL TEXT ALERT: Happy summer! Sorry for the late text but we want to let everyone know that our essay contest winner is Vishal Gobin! We had hoped to announce this earlier but there were so many outstanding

entries to read! The Jennie's gift certificate will be sent to Vishal at home. Have a safe, happy, fabulous summer! See you in September. #YorkvilleUnited

PARTY PARTY PARTY

(P) (C) (G) (V)

GABRIELLE

OMG where r u guys

Vishal won the essay contest!!!!!

I wonder what he wrote!!!!!

He is never serious...
😂 😜 😝 😛 😊 🐵 😈 💩

Cecily, Mara

MARA

Sorry I cut off the conv

People were totes eavesdropping

CECILY

That's ok

MARA

Can we talk over text now

CECILY

Um ok 😏😏😏

I think my mom snoops but I will delete conv 📱➡️📵

MARA

Haha same

CECILY

Did I freak u out 😱😬😐😮😵😵

MARA

No

CECILY

R u sure

MARA

Did u know I have 2 aunts

I mean bc they r married

CECILY

No

MARA

Oh

CECILY

Ok it is weird to text u but I can see ur expressions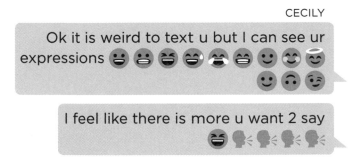

I feel like there is more u want 2 say

MARA

Yeah kinda

CECILY

Soo?

MARA

I'm just not sure I like u like that and I am so sorry

I like how we r really good friends tho

I still like 2 hang w/ u so much

CECILY

Ok me 2

MARA

U look really sad

I am so sorry

CECILY

Igg, Mara

Brb

Guys, please help

P C G

Guys, please meet me in Pri's room

Need 2 talk to u

GABRIELLE

Umm r u ok

PRIANKA

Coming

PARTY PARTY PARTY

VICTORIA

Where r u guys 🎈!??

CAKE

P   C   G   K   N

KIMBERLY

Cake in 5 min 🌀🍰🎂

Vic's mom wants 2 know ???

Where is every1 ??

UR THE BEST, CECE, PLEASE DON'T CRY

PRIANKA

Ok we have 2 go down 4 cake 🎂🍰🍥🥞

Sorry conv got cut short ⌛⌛⌛⌛

Can text 4 a min as we walk but b careful

GABRIELLE

Cece, I am so sorry ur hurt 😳😩🐱

Bc ur the best ever 💕💞😍😘😻👊😝

CECILY

Luv u guys so much 💜💜💜💜💌💜

PRIANKA

TBH everything makes so much more sense now 👍👍👍

GABRIELLE

LOL, Pri 😝😁😅😀😹

PRIANKA

Who cares who u like ❓❓

Boys girls whatev 👦👦👦👧👧👧

It's all good 👌👌

CECILY

Thank u 🙏🙏🙏

GABRIELLE

I agree 💟💟

Love every1 ❤️❤️❤️💝❤️💟💝💜💞

CECILY

Ha 😼😼

PRIANKA

TBH boys r kinda dumb 🤦🤦🤦

I love them anyway 😻😻😻😻😻

Just not Vishal 👨💻🚫⛔

192

But know it all Jared is kinda cute 👶

GABRIELLE

I thought u hated him and his KIA-ness 👀
🫤 👀 🫤 🫤 👀

PRIANKA

Yeah I kinda do 🫤

Love hate whatevs 🙅‍♀️ 💑 🫤

CECILY

Can't believe Vish won essay contest
🖊️ 🖋️ 📝 ✏️

PRIANKA

ME NEITHER 🖥️ 🚫 ⛔

I kinda want him 2 send 2 me 🖥️

GABRIELLE

Ooooh 👏 👏 👏 👏

PRIANKA

Not forwarding 🚫 ⛔ 🚫 ⛔ 🔟

Staying safe 👌👌

If he sends u can read on my 📱➡️📱

CECILY

Ok ✔️

Kinda 🙁 😮 I didn't win

PRIANKA

U can't win everything @ school, Cece 📗 📗 📗 📗 📚

Would be awk 😳 😈 😈 👹 🐵 🤡

CECILY

Yeah true 💁 💁 💁

PRIANKA

K cake time 🎂 🍰 🌀 🌀 🍰 🎂

CECILY

Luv you guys 💕 💌 😻 😍

have a super fab amazing summer and come
back in September and crush 7th grade

enjoy the sunshine and warm weather and
NO HOMEWORK! WOOOOOOO HOOOOO

SCHOOL'S OUT FOR SUMMER! YAYYYYYY!!!!
HAVE SO MUCH FUN! ENJOY EVERY SECOND!
SUMMER IS THE BEST BEST BEST BEST BEST!
YAYAYAYYAYAYAYAYAYYAYAAYAYAYYA

EAT ICE CREAM EVERY DAYYYYYYY!

SWIM A TON! AND HAVE SO
MUCH FUN!

Prianka, Gabrielle

PRIANKA

Ok these messages r kinda silly 😊😄😂😅😎😟😔🤔🤗😐😑😐🙄😶😐😐

But fun right? 😈👿🤠🤑🤕😴👿👹👺💩

GABRIELLE

Yeah 👍

Hey Gabs,
i didn't get to see you @
the end of the party so i
am writing you this note and
dropping in your mailbox on
my way home.

   Just wanted to say it was
fun hanging out with you this
year. Have an amazing time
on your camping trip.

   See you in seventh grade.
   Peace,
   Colin

OMG

GABRIELLE

Guys, Colin put a note in my 📫📪📫

PRIANKA

Like a love note? 💌💌💌

CECILY

Ooooh

GABRIELLE

IDK but I think I love him again 💕💕💕 💕

VICTORIA

LOL did u talk @ the party

GABRIELLE

No I chickened out 🐔🍗🐔🍗

VICTORIA

Ok so whatevs

Yeah will see what happens in Sept

Vishal, Prianka

PRIANKA

I didn't get 2 say congrats on the essay

VISHAL

Thx

PRIANKA

I'm still happy 4 u

VISHAL

IK

Ur emojis r annoying

Can u stop

PRIANKA

Sure

Sorry if u hate me now

VISHAL

Might be awk when we're in India now u know

PRIANKA

It will be ok

VISHAL

Whatever

Ur so weird

PRIANKA

IK

I like being weird

VISHAL

Fine

PRIANKA

Can I read yr essay

VISHAL

LOL no

U tell me u don't like me anymore & then
want to read my essay

Hahahahahahahahahahhahahahah

PRIANKA

Fine bye

They may post online anyway

VISHAL

Maybe

Bye

Dear Cecily,

You ran off at the party and then I only saw you from afar. I was going to send this in an email but since you live next door it was just easier to write it and drop it off.

I'm really sorry about the way things ended at the party. I'm so glad you felt comfortable enough to talk to me. And I still really think you're amazing and a fabulous friend. I don't want things to change between us. I just don't know how I feel about anything love related. I don't like boys or girls—I am just kind of here waiting to figure out how I feel. It's kind of odd but it's the truth.

I hope you have an amazing summer.

See you soon.

Love,

Mara ☺

Cecily, Mara

C M

MARA

Did u get my note

CECILY

Yeah

MARA

Ok just wanted 2 make sure

Have the best summer

CECILY

U 2

MARA

CECILY

SUMMMERRRRRRRRR

P C G V

PRIANKA

Guys good morning!

1st morning of summer break

We need 2 celebrate 🎉🎉😀

GABRIELLE

Good morning 😎😎😎

U just woke me up 🐱😬

Was excited 2 sleep in 😴😭🛏️

PRIANKA

Oops sorry 😬🙄😮😦

Meet @ Martin's 4 breakfast in 1 hr 🍞🍳
🥓🥓

K sounds fab 🌾🌾🌾🌾🌾🌾🌾🌾

I want some fresh squeezed OJ 🍎 🍎

GABRIELLE

Ooooh me 2 👍

VICTORIA

C u there

Kim & Nic just left

I want pancakes 🥞🥞🥞🥞🥞🥞🥞
🥞🥞🥞🥞

CECILY

Yummmmmm 😻😻😻😻

PRIANKA

Fab way 2 start summer rite 👏 👏 👏

GABRIELLE

Totes 👍 👍

Getting ready

HERE WE COME SUMMER

VICTORIA

Yeahhhhhh

PRIANKA

Yessssssssss LOL PANCAKES
🥞🥞🥞🥞🥞🥞🥞🥞🥞🥞🥞

Can that be r new group name

CECILY

Hahahaha sure

No matter what we call rselves - this is gonna b the best summer everrrrrrrr 😎

PRIANKA

BC we are the BEST FRIENDS EVER!!!!!!!!!
👭👭👭

GABRIELLE

CECILY

GLOSSARY

2 to

2gether together

4 for

4eva forever

4get forget

any1 anyone

awk awkward

bc because

BFF best friends forever

BFFAE best friends forever and ever

b-room bathroom

b/t between

c see

caf cafeteria

comm committee

COMO crying over missing out

comp computer

DEK don't even know

deets details

def definitely

diff different

disc discussion

emo emotional

every1 everyone

fab fabulous

fabolicious extra fabulous

fac faculty

fave favorite

Fla Florida

FOMO fear of missing out

fone phone

fyi for your information

gd god

gtg gotta go

gn good night

gnight good night

gr8 great

hw homework

ICB I can't believe

IDC I don't care

IDEK I don't even know

IDK I don't know

IHNC I have no clue

IK I know

ILY I love you

ILYSM I love you so much

JK just kidding

K OK

KIA know-it-all

L8r later

LMK let me know

lol laugh out loud

luv love

n e way anyway

NM nothing much

nvm never mind

nums numbers

obv obviously

obvi obviously

obvs obviously

OMG oh my God

ooc out of control

peeps people

perf perfect

pgs pages

plzzzz please

pos possibly

q question

r are / our

ridic ridiculous

rlly really

RN right now

sci science

sec second

sem semester

scheds schedules

shud should

some1 someone

SWAK sealed with a kiss

TBH to be honest

thx thanks

TMI too much information

tm tomorrow

tmrw tomorrow

tomrw tomorrow

tomw tomorrow

totes totally

u you

ur your

vv very, very

w/ with

wb write back

w/o without

WIGO what is going on

whatev whatever

wknd weekend

WTH what the heck

wud would

wut what

wuzzzz what's

Y why

ACKNOWLEDGMENTS

Extra-special thanks to Maria Barbo & Stephanie Guerdan @ KT Books for all their sparkly, wonderful ideas. Thanks to Alyssa Eisner Henkin for being a superstar agent. Thank you, Katherine, Aurora, Amy, Bethany, Ann, and all the fab peeps at Katherine Tegen Books for all your hard work. To all my readers: ur the best! ✳ ✳ 🎆 🎇 ILYSM! Thanks to Dave, Aleah, Hazel, the Greenwalds, the Rosenbergs & the BWL library tech team for all of the support. Last but def not least, thanks to Gabi and Sophia for coming up with the title. 💕 🖤 💕 🖤

LISA GREENWALD lives in NYC 🍎 w/ her husband & 2 young daughters 👨 👩 👧 👧. She 💜s: 😎 📚 🏃 & 🎬. Summer is her favorite season ☀️ 🌞 🍉 🍧 🍦 📖 🕶️. Visit her 💻 @ www.lisagreenwald.com.

Don't miss Lisa Greenwald's
Friendship List series!

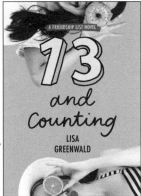

Are you ready for more CPG4Eva?
Don't miss *TBH #4: IDK What's Next*!